Dedication

This book is dedicated to Amy. With love and thanks for putting up with my endless hours of thinking about things.

Leadership from A to Z

Words for leaders to lean on

BEN COSH

Copyright © 2022 Ben Cosh
All rights reserved

Foreword

For the past few years, I've been running the YouTube channel *Leadership with Mike*. I've been lucky enough to get more than 1.5 million views as of writing this foreword.

In the building of my channel, I was on the search for other leaders who had a similar philosophy as I do. Where we look at leadership as a bunch of simple tasks and ideas.

One of the people I was blessed to meet is the author of this book, Ben Cosh.

Ben is the definition of Gentleman and a Scholar.

He has such a great understanding of leadership and is able to simplify complex issues that can arise for leaders.

I know this firsthand as Ben has become one of my "go-to" advisors when I have leadership questions.

When Ben told me about his leadership book and how it was a simple breakdown from A to Z, I was so excited.

Not only to cheer on a friend but because I knew if anyone was going to breakdown leadership into simple words and meanings, it would be Ben.

As I said, Ben is one of the people I turn to when I need help simplifying leadership. You will see why as you dive into this book.

The whole philosophy on my leadership channel is "no nonsense sense". I like clear answers without any fluff.

If that's what you're looking for, then I can promise you, you will find it in this book.

Getcha Kaffee and enjoy the read!

Mike Ashie
Leadership with Mike
mikeashie.com

Introduction

This is a crowd-sourced book.

It started with a game played in a social media group about leadership.

I challenged the group to come up with three words describing leadership, all starting with the same letter, and wondered aloud if we could do the whole alphabet.

I started the ball rolling with Engage, Enthuse, Empower.

In just a few hours we had gone through the whole alphabet with contributions totalling 170 words from all over the world.

I gathered those contributions and used them to write a collection of short meditations on leadership, one for each letter of the alphabet, based on the words brought forward by the community.

These first took life as a series of short videos on YouTube.

And now they're in this book.

As you deal with the daily challenges of leadership, I hope these short reflections will give you something to lean on.

Maybe you'll find a new thought, or a reminder of something you've known for years.

Maybe one of the words will make you feel better on a difficult day. Or give you something new and exciting to focus on.

However you use this short leadership dictionary, I'm delighted to share it with you.

Ben Cosh

PS: I've created an exclusive free gift for you at

leadershipjetway.com/bookbonus

Grab it now to instantly upgrade your leadership!

A

Ambition, Aspirational, Assertive, Approachable, Amicable, Achieve

Every leader needs AMBITION.

You've got to think you can change the world and make it better. For your team, your colleagues and your customers.

You've got to believe you can do something good and make a difference.

That starts when you have ambition for your team and when you're ASPIRATIONAL enough that you can sell it to the people around you and inspire them to greatness.

Sometimes you need to be ASSERTIVE.

We can shy away from it, but often you have to push hard to overcome objections, go against the prevailing wisdom, or fight the inertia of the organisation.

And on the other side of the coin…

You need to be APPROACHABLE and AMICABLE as well.

Your people need to know they can come to you with difficulties and that you'll be understanding and supportive. Not dismissive and cold.

Support your team and you'll ACHIEVE incredible things.

B

Brave, Bright, Brilliant

Leaders have to be BRAVE.

You must be willing to speak your mind, even if it goes against the grain.

Actually. Especially if it goes against the grain.

It's easy to say the things that everyone's thinking. And usually unnecessary.

Much harder, and much more important, to say the things no-one else is thinking and raise the issues everyone else avoids. That takes bravery.

So does making difficult decisions. You need the courage to do things when it's risky. And to say no when agreeing would be easier.

Leaders are often BRIGHT and BRILLIANT.

You need the ability to think through complex stuff and figure out how to handle it.

And you need to be a shining light when times are tough.

Your team will look to you to show them it'll be OK and to help them steer a way through.

C

Clarity, Challenging, Confidence, Consistent, Commitment, Considerate, Caring

Above all else, leaders must bring CLARITY to complex situations.

Boil away the irrelevant, the marginal and the less-important. Get to the crux of the matter.

Find the thing that affects us most and work out what to do about it.

Leaders must be CHALLENGING.

Challenge the status quo. Especially if it isn't working.

Challenge lazy, rushed, or incomplete thinking from your team or elsewhere in the hierarchy.

Challenge yourself and those around you to do your very best work and be the most impactful people you can be.

You must have CONFIDENCE to do this. In yourself. And in your team.

You must have CONSISTENT COMMITMENT to the pursuit of your most important priorities.

Be consistent in how you deal with colleagues, and committed to your combined success.

And you must be CONSIDERATE and CARING to your colleagues, clients and customers!

D

Dedication, Determination, Devotion, Diligence, Dependable, Deliberate, Dignified, Decisive, Details, Dexterous, Delightful, Done

Leaders need DEDICATION, DETERMINATION, DEVOTION and DILIGENCE.

Your people need to know you're pulling for them.

Your organisation needs to know you're focused on pushing things forward and making things better.

They both need to know you're putting in the hours, working the priorities, focused on your combined success.

Try to be DEPENDABLE, DELIBERATE and DIGNIFIED.

I would choose these three all the time.

I'd prefer to work with a leader that is thoughtful and measured, over one who is fiery, frenzied and frantic.

It is through making decisions and acting on them that everything gets done.

So you must be DECISIVE.

Even if there are lots of intricate DETAILS and you need highly DEXTEROUS thinking to handle them.

And you might as well try to be DELIGHTFUL about it.

There's usually room for a smile and an uplifting word.

It can make all the difference to your colleagues.

And to finish… Sometimes, you're just DONE!

That's OK. You need to rest. Breathe. Recharge.

You can't lead if you're broken and exhausted.

E

Empathy, Engage, Enthuse, Encourage, Excellence, Empower, Enriching

Leaders need EMPATHY.

You have to be able to put yourself in someone else's shoes so you can recognise, validate and value their emotions and energy levels.

Because it is only by understanding others that you will be able to…

ENGAGE, ENTHUSE and ENCOURAGE them to deliver EXCELLENCE.

For themselves, and their team.

This is a much better approach than directing and controlling, while only caring about the numbers and KPIs on your spreadsheet.

Great leaders EMPOWER their teams.

Read David Marquet's brilliant book Turn the Ship Around to hear about doing this in the most high-pressured environments.

Move from leader-follower to leader-leader and you'll be pouring jetfuel into your business engine.

And ENRICHING your team as you go.

F

Freedom, Fair, Free, Fear, Frugal, Faith, Forgiving, Forward, Future, Fulfilled

So many great leaders have called for and brought about greater FREEDOM.

If you can create an environment for your team that is FAIR and FREE of FEAR they will thank you for it.

Leaders have to be FRUGAL.

You have to make the most effective and efficient use of the resources you have available.

You have to be ruthless in prioritising your time.

You have to set boundaries on your time and availability.

Be careful though, because leaders also need to be generous and giving. But that's a discussion for the next chapter.

Things won't always go quite as you expect them to.

So leaders must have FAITH in their vision, be FORGIVING to their colleagues and themselves, and keep everyone's eyes FORWARD.

Because it's in working together with an eye on the FUTURE that you'll build a team that is FULFILLED.

G

Great, Go-getter, Graceful, Guide, Goals, Generous, Give, Gain

GREAT leaders are GO-GETTERS, who want to make things happen for their teams.

They move and shake.

They see opportunities and go after them.

But they remain GRACEFUL under pressure, staying on top of priorities, communicating skillfully and looking in control.

If you hold on to your temper and measure your emotions you'll be a better GUIDE when things don't go as planned.

And guiding is what leaders do.

They understand what's going on, they set the GOALS, and then chart a course to steer the team towards success.

We saw in the last chapter that leaders must be frugal.

But you should also be GENEROUS.

GIVE your time, your challenge and your support. Encourage your team to give to each other and your customers.

Because actually… The more you give as a leader, the more you'll GAIN in the end.

H

Humble, Honest, Hardworking, Heroism, Hope, Happy, Help, Heights

Yes. Leaders must be confident in their decisions.

But you have to be HUMBLE enough to recognise that not everyone thinks like you do.

Take the time to listen to other voices.

Understand other perspectives. And sharpen your own understanding by doing so.

Leaders must be HONEST. About the things they know, and the things they don't.

Sometimes you can't tell your team everything. Be honest about that too.

HARDWORKING leaders bring their teams with them.

But be wary of HEROISM.

Fight for your team. For your vision. For your integrity.

Act in ways that make your team look to you for HOPE in moments of difficulty.

But the hero who tries to solve all the problems leaves their team no room to grow and excel, while burning themselves out.

And remember… Shawn Achor teaches that happiness is a cause of success. Not a result of it.

So be a HAPPY leader and you'll HELP your team reach great HEIGHTS!

I

Integrity, Inquiry, Invite, Ideas, Interest, Innovate, Initiate, Inspire, Implement, Invest, Influence, Impact

Lead with INTEGRITY and a spirit of INQUIRY.

Act with consistency and honesty. Ask questions. Seek first to understand, then be understood.

INVITE comment and IDEAS from your team.

Be INTERESTED in their thoughts and in them as people.

Then INNOVATE.

Leadership is about finding new ways to do things, or new things to do, that make the world a little bit better.

So INITIATE change.

INSPIRE your colleagues to IMPLEMENT their ideas.

INVEST your time in supporting them.

Do all these things and you'll grow your INFLUENCE and IMPACT as a leader.

J

Just, Jocularity, Joke, Joyful

Leaders must be JUST.

Adjudicate disputes with consistency and an eye on both the rules and plain good sense.

But don't be too gloomy.

There is usually room for a smile and touch of JOCULARITY.

Just be careful what you choose to JOKE about.

And when the team wins, make it a JOYFUL occasion.

K

Knowledge, Keen, Kind

So much of Leadership is based on KNOWLEDGE.

Knowing what's going on.

Knowing what your team thinks and feels.

Knowing what works. And what doesn't.

Knowing who to turn to for help.

Knowing when to keep pushing.

And knowing when to rest.

You must be KEEN.

Keen-eyed. Keen-minded.

And keen to see your team succeed and your vision become reality.

But be KIND.

Remember your team are people. Not widget-making machines.

Get to KNOW them. Keep them keen. And you'll keep winning!

L

Look, Listen, Learn, Leap, Legitimacy, Long-suffering, Live, Love, Leading

Leaders need to LOOK, LISTEN and LEARN before they LEAP.

Watch what's happening in the world.

Take deliberate steps to hear from your team.

Find out how they feel before making your moves and you'll build LEGITIMACY with your people.

The leader can be LONG-SUFFERING.

Taking a little less than your share of the credit and a little more of your share of the responsibility over and over again can be tiring.

So you must remember to LIVE too. Not just for your business and your team. But for yourself and your family.

And lastly… LOVE.

This is a word that can be uncomfortable.

But everything comes back to it in the end.

Acting from a place of love.

LEADING from a place of love.

It's always the right thing to do.

M

Manage, Meticulous, Mission, Master, Morals, Motivator, Mentor, Magnanimous, Magic

Leaders have to MANAGE.

So many people will tell you "management" and "leadership" are enemies.

They're not. They're dance partners.

Most leaders have to do management as well as leadership.

You have to make sure stuff gets done, gets done right and gets done on time.

The trick is to make sure you keep leadership and management in balance and working together (not against each other).

Leaders must be METICULOUS over details, while never losing sight of the MISSION and the big picture.

You have to MASTER your own MORALS, intentions and actions, before you can hope to be a MOTIVATOR and MENTOR to your team.

And you have to be MAGNANIMOUS when things don't go so well.

Or when someone grabs a little more than their share of the credit.

Do all of this well… and you'll make MAGIC things happen.

N

Noble, Needed, Negotiate, Nasty, Nice, Natural, Nurturing

Leadership is a NOBLE calling.

Serving others, lifting them up, helping them see priorities and possibilities.

Making positive change happen.

Leaders are NEEDED everywhere.

Leaders must NEGOTIATE to achieve win-win outcomes and gain the resources their team needs to thrive.

But you don't have to be NASTY.

There's always room to be NICE.

And be NATURAL.

If you are authentically you, your team will recognise and appreciate it.

They will let you in, so that you can be NUTURING as you work together for success.

O

Observant, Objective, Organised, Optimistic, Oriented

Leaders must be OBSERVANT.

Part of finding your "vision" for the future is seeing what's happening now.

You need to understand what's going on before you can work out what needs to happen and set OBJECTIVES.

Oh… And be OBJECTIVE in working out your priorities and tracking your progress.

Leaders must be ORGANISED.

Know what your priorities are.

Have systems to handle the small stuff, so you can focus on the big stuff.

And stay OPTIMISTIC.

Even if the circumstances are tough, leaders must look to the future with hope.

Set a positive vision that your colleagues can see themselves in and keep them ORIENTED towards it.

P

Purpose, Punctual, Polite, Patient, Passionate, Participation, Priorities, Productive

Leaders must have PURPOSE. For themselves and for their team.

You must be PUNCTUAL and POLITE.

It's just basic good manners. If you can't get that sorted… how do you expect anyone else to do so?

But be PATIENT too.

People are people. Not robots.

Mistakes happen. Things take time to improve.

Give space and room for people to grow.

Leaders must be PASSIONATE!

It's the best way to encourage PARTICIPATION and real buy-in.

Care about what you're doing.

Make sure you're doing work that matters by setting PRIORITIES and being ruthless in your focus on them.

Because then you, and your team, will be truly PRODUCTIVE.

Q

Quality, Questions, Quotable

Leaders must set the standard for QUALITY.

Call on your colleagues to strive for excellence.

Leaders must ask QUESTIONS.

How are you? How are things going? How can I help?

Don't let received wisdom, or the way we've always done things hold you back.

Ask why things are done the way they are. Ask if we can do them better.

And if you can, be QUOTABLE.

Speak in ways that resonate.

Say things simply, so that people can understand quickly.

If they remember what you've said, they might remember to act on it!

R

Rigorous, Rigours, Resilience, Respect, Responsibility, Resourceful, Results

Leaders must be RIGOROUS.

In their attention to detail and their pursuit of big picture aims.

And they must be ready to tackle the RIGOURS of leadership.

It can be lonely and exhausting, with constantly shifting demands and circumstances.

So leaders need to build their RESILIENCE.

Set your mindset away from victim-think, prioritise ruthlessly and pay attention to your health and wellbeing.

Leaders must RECOGNISE and RESPECT the different experiences and talents and viewpoints of their people.

Take RESPONSIBILITY for ensuring your team gets where they need to be.

But empower them rather than ordering them around.

Be RESOURCEFUL when challenges arise.

Come up with new ways to do things, stay hopeful and keep your team looking forwards.

Do all these things and you're bound to get RESULTS.

S

Sensitive, Steer, Sensible, Symphony, Synthesis, Success, Sacrifices, Smile

Leaders need to be SENSITIVE to what's going on around them in order to STEER a course for the team.

Figure out what's happening in the business, in your sector, in the economy and society more widely.

Work out what it all means for your team and pick a direction.

While also being SENSITIVE to how your people will react.

Be SENSIBLE.

Wild and crazy ideas have their place.

It is good to be bold and take decisions quickly.

But don't carry your team over a cliff edge.

Leadership is like conducting a great SYMPHONY orchestra.

Weaving together the talents of individual musicians into a SYNTHESIS of sound that carries the listener forward.

Leaders must align their teams, keep them focused on a common goal and fuse their talents into SUCCESS.

Often, leaders must make SACRIFICES along the way.

Sometimes the hours are long and the tasks demanding.

But there is usually room for a SMILE and a sense of humour along the way.

Don't forget to be human and show it from time to time.

T

Timely, Team, Trainable, Truth, Tactful, Trust, Tired, Tenacity

Leaders must be TIMELY.

Don't procrastinate. Decide.

Catch the moment and move your TEAM forward.

And your TEAM isn't just the group that reports to you. It's whoever you're working with at that moment.

Whether you're the most senior person, or the most junior, you can lead from wherever you are. And real leaders always do.

Leaders should let themselves be TRAINABLE.

I've been doing leadership for 15 years and I learn something new (or realise I need to learn something new) every single day.

Let your team train you on how they feel, what they think, what they need.

Seek out training that makes you a better leader.

Tell the TRUTH, but be TACTFUL, and you will build TRUST.

There will be times when you're TIRED. Leadership can be hard.

But it's also so rewarding.

So keep at it. Show some TENACITY!

U

Understanding, Utilitarian, Utilise, Unsung, Uplifting, Upwards

Leaders must be UNDERSTANDING.

You have to understand what's going on, so you can figure out what needs to happen and work with people to make it happen.

And you have to understand the people you work with.

They're people not robots. And they have all the mess in their lives and their heads that everybody has.

Leaders must be UTILITARIAN.

Focus on being useful.

On actually getting stuff done and serving people well.

Not appearing to get stuff done and looking flashy while you do it.

UTILISE the talents of your team in pursuit of your purpose and goals.

Remember that leaders must often let themselves be UNSUNG.

You have to take a little less than your share of the credit. (And a little more than your share of the blame.)

And in moments of difficulty, leaders must be UPLIFTING.

Turn your team's eyes, minds and hearts away from how tough things are, and towards how you're going to move forwards, onwards and UPWARDS!

V

Vicarious, Victories, Vivacious, Vitality, Vulnerability, Visible

Leaders should be VICARIOUS.

Live your successes and VICTORIES through the eyes and achievements of your team.

Be VIVACIOUS and bring VITALITY to your workplace.

Keep the energy up. Keep it positive. Keep it happy.

Don't be afraid to show some VULNERABILITY.

Not too much.

But reminding your team you are human will enhance relationships and make it more likely that they will bring their vulnerabilities to you.

And be VISIBLE.

You're the leader.

It's difficult to lead from a hideaway office.

Be out in front, or in amongst the troops, or behind them cheering them on.

But make sure they know you're there.

W

Wilful, Wisdom, Worthy, Work, Win

Leaders must be WILFUL.

You have to know where you're trying to get to, and have the strength of mind and purpose to see it through.

Always try to lead with WISDOM.

Yes. Make decisions and move forwards.

But think carefully.

Weigh your choices and the impact on those around you.

And be WORTHY of the responsibility placed on you as a leader, of the trust placed in you by your team.

Stand up for what's right.

WORK hard.

And you'll WIN.

X

Xenophile, Xenomorphic, Xanadite

You should aim to be a XENOPHILE. Someone who is accepting and welcoming of others.

In this globalised, diversified world leaders must draw strength from how we experience and do things differently and make us all better in the process.

Leaders must be XENOMORPHIC. Able to adopt or adapt to culture.

If you try to make changes or impose a brand new culture on day one, you'll probably fail.

Instead, immerse yourself in the culture that already exists.

Learn how things are done around here.

Figure out the personalities and processes.

Then, if things need moving, do it from the inside, with patience and time.

And lastly, be a XANADITE. Someone who lives in contentment and sees beauty in everything.

What a wonderful goal for leaders, and for all of us, to have!

Y

Yardstick, Yearning, Yielder, Yourself

Be a YARDSTICK for your team.

Show them where the edges are.

Help them measure the distance from where we are now to where we'd like to be.

Leaders must have a deep YEARNING to achieve the goals and fulfil the purpose of their teams.

A loose hope that something can be done just won't cut it.

Be a YIELDER.

Not one who gives up at the first sign of trouble.

But who yields responsibility and empowerment to your team.

And most of all… be YOURSELF.

Authenticity, the art of being truly you, is perhaps the most important leadership characteristic of all.

Acting like you think a leader should, but in ways that don't fit your true personality, is a recipe for disaster.

Your team will feel something isn't right, think you're being fake and lose trust in you.

Your own version of you is enough. Don't hide it. Lean into it.

Z

Zappy, Zazzy, Zealous

Leaders can be ZAPPY and ZAZZY!

Well. Don't take it too far.

But be positive and upbeat.

And don't be afraid to be bold and charismatic if that suits your natural style.

And always be ZEALOUS.

Be zealous in pursuit of your vision for a better future.

Run hard towards your goals and fight for the success of your team.

And be zealous in developing yourself to be the best leader you can be.

What next?

Visit: leadershipjetway.com/bookbonus

I've put together an exclusive free gift to thank you for buying this book.

In this short video training and collection of downloads you'll learn my favourite four words in this book and how to use them every day to upgrade your leadership instantly.

Grab it now to be a more confident, capable leader.

leadershipjetway.com/bookbonus

Thanks

This book wouldn't exist without the people who played my little word game on social media.

Ahmed H, Bilgin, Bodhi S, Cindy C-M, Cole R, Denise T, Dipti, Eleanor M, Grace Q, Isabella M, Jane Z, Jason W, Jenny F, John B, Kim M, Mahfuzur R, Manuel B, Mariette E, Mary B, Nesrine Y, Raja S, Raluca S, Sarita Y, Shadrach B, Shane W, Tan EG, Tino A, Tonis L, Vikki E

And especially John R for the Xs!

Thank you for inspiring me to write.

I'm grateful to Mike Ashie for his kind Foreword. To Ian MacLeod and Paul Banoub, for reviewing the manuscript and offering encouragement and high fives. And to all three of them for inspiring me every day with their leadership content and commitment to helping people be better.

Most of all I'm grateful to you for buying and reading this book.

Please do come and get your free gift at:

leadershipjetway.com/bookbonus

About the author

Ben Cosh has been in leadership roles since 2004. He has grown from line-managing a team of one, to board level positions running departments of 300 people.

When he isn't reading about, writing about or doing leadership, he is a husband, father, mathematician, and musician.

At leadershipjetway.com Ben provides resources, courses and coaching to help new and experienced leaders upgrade their leadership skills and impact.

Upgrade your leadership instantly with an exclusive free gift available at:

leadershipjetway.com/bookbonus

Printed in Great Britain
by Amazon